MY FIRST

EASTER
BOOK

by Annetta E. Dellinger
illustrated by Linda Hohag

created by The Child's World

CHILDRENS PRESS ™

CHICAGO

Library of Congress Cataloging in Publication Data

Dellinger, Annetta E.
  My first Easter book.

    Summary: Poems describe various aspects of Easter,
such as coloring eggs, spring weather, new clothes,
and an Easter parade.
    1. Easter—Juvenile poetry.   2. Children's poetry,
American.   [1. Easter—Poetry.   2. American poetry]
I. Hohag, Linda, ill.   II. Child's World (Firm)
III. Title.
PS3554.E4439M9 1985   811'.54   84-21512
ISBN 0-516-02904-5

MY FIRST

EASTER
BOOK

Easter

It's here, my favorite time of year,
          EASTER!
I love . . .
     watching fluffy baby chicks,
     seeing birds make nests with sticks,
     picking flowers as they sprout,
     seeing new life all about!

Grass

Little blades of grass,
   now that you've taken off
   your rough, brown, winter coat
   and put on your new,
   green, spring jacket,
   I want to run and
         j u m p
   and feel your softness.
And you can tickle my toes!

Gifts of Easter

I like the gifts that Easter brings. . .
   colored eggs,
     grass that greens,
  new spring clothes,
    jelly beans,
  pretty flowers that unfold,
    the message that is told.
There's new life in spring.

Easter Egg Tree

As I was walking
d
o
w
n
the street,
I saw the strangest sight.
Easter eggs of every color
were sparkling in the light.
Some were orange,
some were red,
others were purple
and pink.
How does Bunny paint them?
With soft tail
and ink?

Daffodil

After a long winter's nap,
  deep,
    deep,
      deep down under the ground,
  the little bulb woke up.
She stretched and stretched her
  green, slender body
  up, up, up to the top of the ground!
"Hello, little green blades of grass;
hello, warm sunshine," she said.
And then she gently lifted
  her soft yellow face
  and swayed in the spring breeze.

Coloring Eggs

Dip it,
   tip it,
      turn it around.
Swirl it,
   twirl it,
      like a merry-go-round.
Coloring eggs is lots of fun,
   count one,
         two,
           three,
and then you're done.

Hunting Eggs

Hunting eggs, I found thirty-two.
My favorite was the
   dark,
   dark blue.
My brother said he liked it too.
What should I do?
It was MY egg
   in MY basket.
But he begged
   and begged.
We traded:
   ten black jelly beans for
   one dark blue egg.

New Life

Funny little caterpillar
eating,
    eating,
        eating.
Tired little caterpillar,
sleeping,
    sleeping,
        sleeping.
Asleep in a cozy bed you lay.
Wake up!
But don't wiggle and squirm.
Now you're a pretty butterfly
  and not a wiggle worm.

Easter Clothes

I look in the mirror
   and whom do I see?
Someone in shiny shoes of white. . .
   a pretty dress just off the rack. . .
   an Easter bonnet with a bow.
Could that be me?
I don't think so.
When I look in the mirror.
   I usually see
      tennies,
      t-shirt,
        and blue jeans, on me!
But . . . I like looking
    this way
      today!

Easter Parade

What's going on?
It looks like a parade,
   but there is no music. . .
   just people going for a walk
   up the street,
   in new clothes,
   on Easter morning.
I think it's an Easter parade!

Ducklings

For Easter
   I got a yellow fuzzy
   duckling
   named Esther.
She quacks all night
   in the bright moonlight,
   and sleeps all day
   when I want to play.
Mom says she's mixed up,
   and thinks I should have gotten
   a pup!

Easter Bouquet

I hid my hands
  in back of me
    so Mother couldn't see.
She asked,
  "Is it long and brown. . .
  a worm that squirms?
  Is it fuzzy and yellow. . .
  a duck that quacks?"
Then I handed her a bouquet
      of jonquils.
She kissed me twice
  and gave me a hug,
  then laughed and said,
  "You even brought a bug!"

Sunrise

"Let's go to the sunrise program,"
  said Mom.
"What's that?" I asked.
On the way, we saw the
  sun just coming up, turning
  the night into day.
We saw flowers opening and
  a pretty butterfly coming
  out of its cocoon.
We heard bells ringing and
  birds singing a
  song of new life.